WOKE

A Field Guide For Utopia Preppers

For TJ and Lukes.
Let's hope this works.

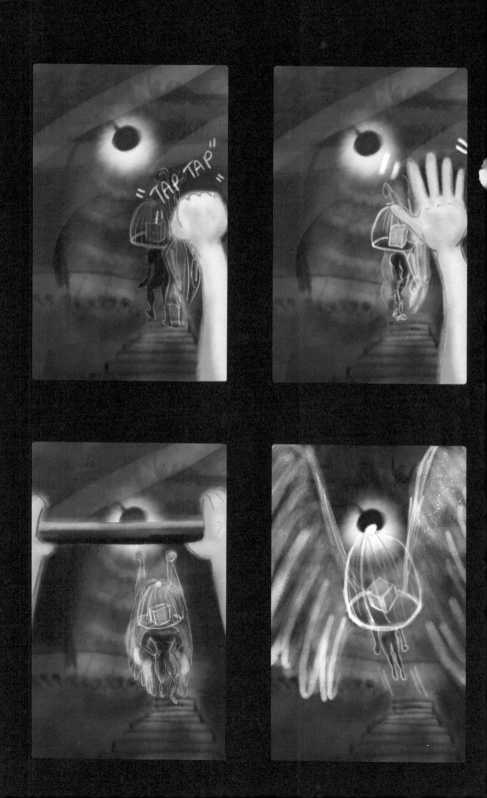

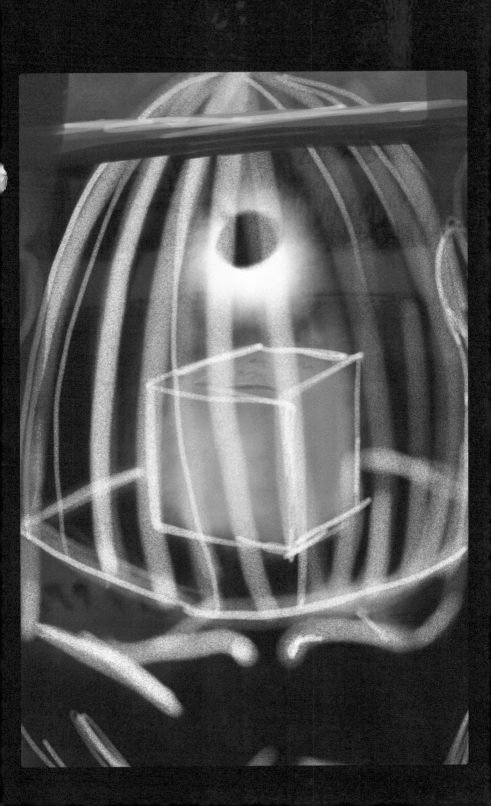

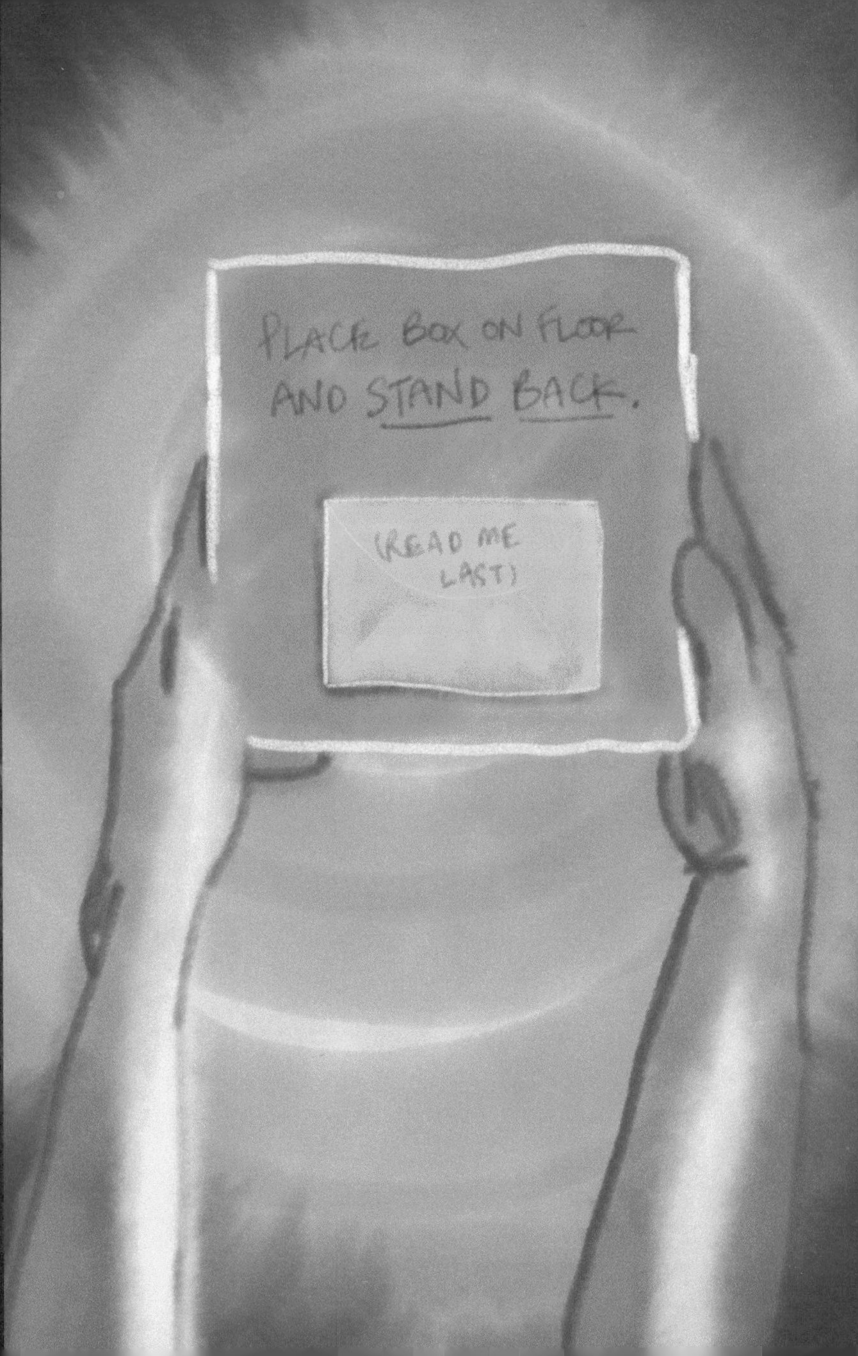
PLACE BOX ON FLOOR
AND STAND BACK.
(READ ME
LAST)

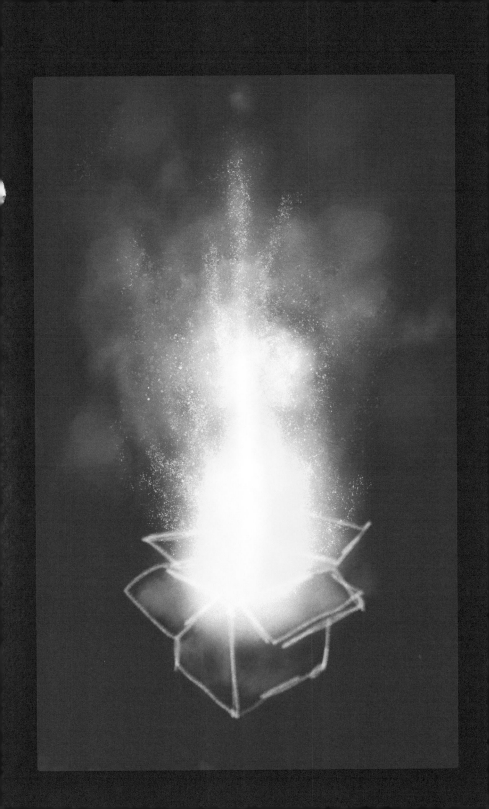

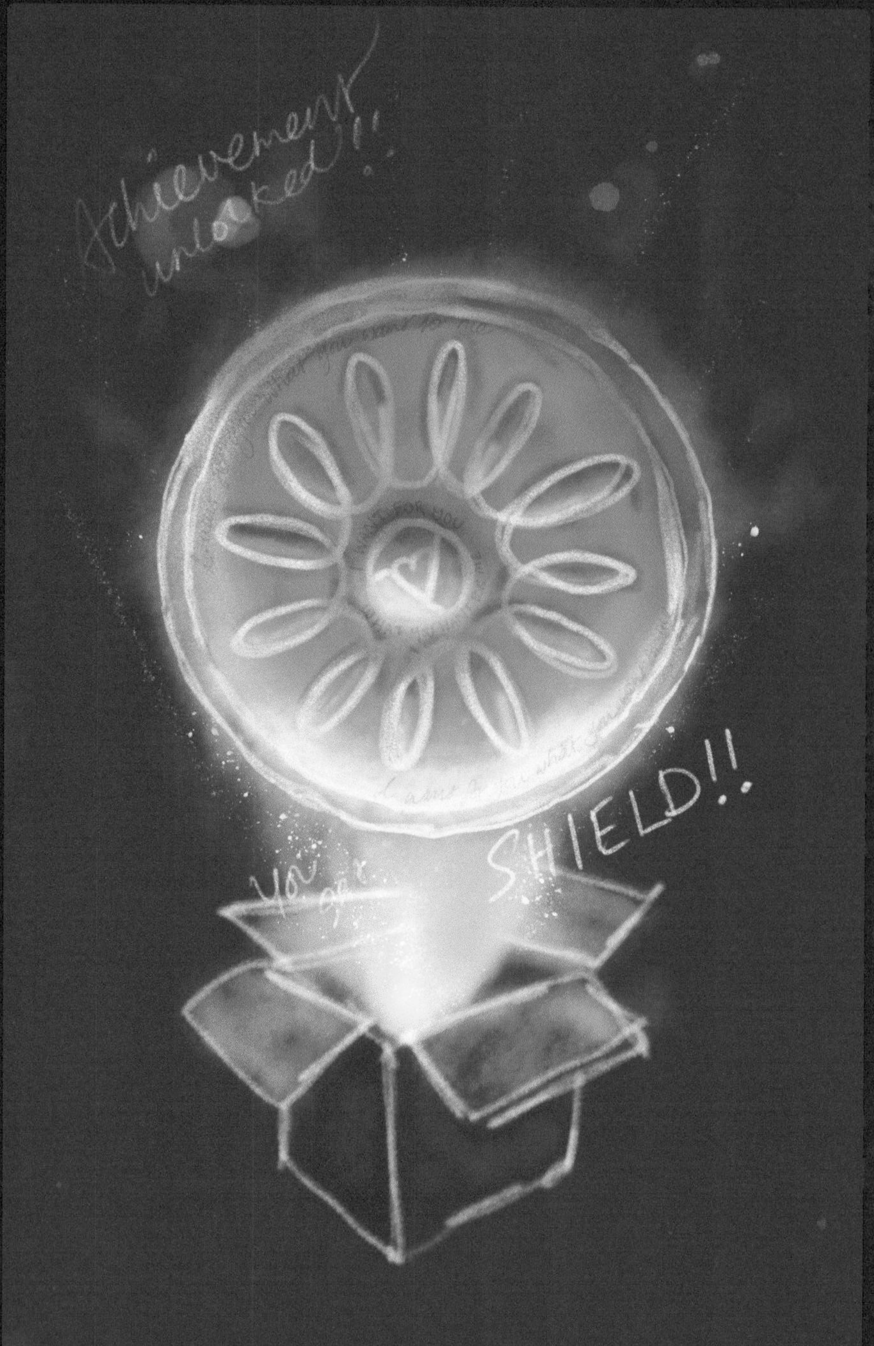
Achievement unlocked!!
You got
SHIELD!!

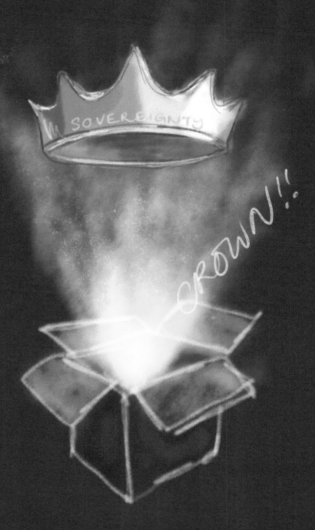

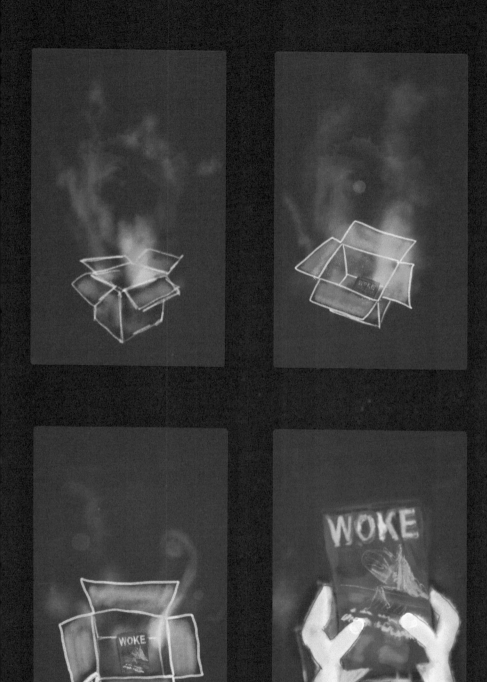

WELCOME

THIS book is for the ones who look with both eyes.

It is not for the right-eye lookers,

who hide away from the pain of the world using comforting ideas

and philosophical positions and spiritual concepts,

who lean back smugly knowing better while the earth screams,

while men in suits with cannibal brains pave over the forests

and coat everything in oil.

The right-eye lookers have killed off that part of themselves which feels,

which cannot look away, which brings them trembling to their knees

at the wet-faced beauty of each instant,

and the wailing of the ocean angels and the tears of the indigenous.

They deftly slip the punches that life throws at their head as it screams

"Look at me! Feel me! Why did you even come here?"

They have traded the aliveness of their lives to avoid the intensity of living.

This book is not for the right-eye lookers.

This book is for the ones who look with both eyes.

It is not for the left-eye lookers,

who behold the flying robots raining fire upon children,

who hear the cries of the mother clutching bloody shreds of nothing,

who feel the dying gasps of the white deer dreamguides

and stand there transfixed by the horror of it all

until they can hardly see for all the tears.

The left-eye lookers lean into each instant,

but the pain consumes them, takes them over, controls them, becomes them.

They build a temple to despondency and begin worshipping strange gods.

Their world has gone gray, and their angels are caged,

and they say it's no good going on.

"We are headed toward doom and so much the better,

for we are all made of poison."

They do not avoid life, and its suffering withers them.

This book is not for the left-eye lookers.

This book is for the ones who look with both eyes.
It is for the ones who see the bombs and the bastards
and stand shaking with the breath of the beast on their skin.
When you look with both eyes, you feel it all,
but you don't flee or freeze.
You fight.
You swing your sword with both hands,
tears pouring from both eyes,
and when they try to drive you back,
you advance.

This book is for the ones who see what is happening,
how strong the beast is, how pervasive its grasp,
how merciless its mission, and say "Fuck it,"
and draw their sword.
For the weeping warriors, for the savage saints,
for the bleeding mothers with fire in their eyes,
for the hidden mystics whose prayers keep the earth spinning,
for the buddhas who'll use their teeth when their blades are broken
and let their evolutionary ancestors howl through them,
this one is for you, my lovelies.

- C

BUY STUFF

Beer
drink beer
drink this kind of beer
because you are thirsty
and because it hurts to be a primate
with an overdeveloped cerebral cortex
on a dying world in a sea of blackness
and because these people are playing volleyball in swimsuits
and drinking beer
BUY STUFF
Buy stuff because your parents never loved you
not really
and because it will make the TV happy
and because everyone understands how to be a person
except you
BUY STUFF

The bone monsters are clicking together
to the shrill canned laughter of '80s sitcoms
and the whales are so full of plastic
that their eyes bulge out like bullfrogs
and the booming fog horns of the garbage barges
say "you are alone"
BUY STUFF
Shut up hippie and go get me a latte
give me your white bison dreamguide
so we can curb stomp it and take its hide
go get a degree and get me a latte
and change into a suit
you've got blood on your clothes
and your wings are almost featherless
BUY STUFF

You are ugly you are ugly

you are ugly you are ugly

as sure as my bones are screaming

and my hands are horrible

and the rainforests are a parking lot

and the pop songs are all the same

and the pop stars are all the same

and the world is coated in crude oil

and the angels are dead

you are ugly

BUY STUFF

so that they'll love you

BUY STUFF

to kill the pain

BUY STUFF

to drown your mother's voice
BUY STUFF
to wage war on the inevitable
BUY STUFF
to hide from your mortality
BUY STUFF
to make the Bastards richer
BUY STUFF
to finally be good enough
BUY STUFF
because it's all they've left you
BUY STUFF
you are alone
BUY STUFF
BUY STUFF

Gold Leaf Donuts
BY RALPH VUITTON

Aspire

GAPS

WHILE the tides rise,

while skullface late night talk show hosts try to make
neoliberalism funny,

while the war drums of the Bastards vibrate the air,

remember:

You are supported by the emptiness between the atoms,

by the emptiness between the stars,

by the emptiness between your thoughts,

by the emptiness which surrounds your perception.

The end has always been as nigh as nigh gets.

Death was lounging between your electrons from the moment
you were conceived.

We who look with both eyes see the gargoyles,

but we also see the emptiness.

We recline against that space between,

cradled in the heart of the timeless.

So when the TV is lying and your friends are all blind,

when they call your light madness and strike your diamond from
your hands,

when Grandmother Tree confesses that she is worried about the
water,

take heart.

Birds of all colors roar out of the darkness in each moment,
join together to form all this,
then fly off.
The needle-toothed Bastards cannot touch your magic,
cannot know the emptiness, cannot see the birds.
A few howling primates gibbering about finance
on a spinning rock that is hurtling through darkness
in a universe that they do not understand.
They do not run this show. They do not lead this dance.

There is a castle at the center of two forest lungs
with a dead angel on a swing made of ivy.
Eel ogres hurl cars in the gaps of your neurons,
and between your electrons,
owls soar.

What I'm trying to say, in my bumbling way,
is that there are so many hiding spaces.
There are miracles lurking in the gaps of all things,
and so little of life is yet known.

I ran into your mother on the underside of a dream,
beneath the hull where the oil bats sleep.
She gave me a sandwich and a necklace of teeth--
oh yeah, and this letter for you in a jug:

Don't be a smartass, don't pick your nose,
and never, ever give up.
This thing will not move how you think it will move;
there's so much more going on than you know.
Say please and thank you and don't bite your friends,
and remember we all love you to death.
You have conjurations of galaxies deep in your guts,
and my child you are covered in feathers.
So listen--Listen!--to those spaces between;
sit and watch until angels march through.
The thing that will save us (don't scratch your butt in public)
will come from the gaps, where the old withered patterns don't
tread.
It will be unexpected, when you're about to give up,
so sit up straight and just do as I say.
Be ready to act, be alert, be polite,
and when the time comes,
let it through.

HE WAS EIGHT AND I WAS NINE

WHEN summers were young we'd go down to the creek
to flip over rocks and look for freshwater squid.
When we found one we'd squeal and squawk
and dare each other to touch it
[no you touch it
no you
I double-dipple dare you
nuh-uh I dare you infinity infinity infinity],
and when the darkness came we'd watch fireflies,
swarms of them,
staring stupefied in their radiance.

"How many do you think there are?" I asked.
"Billions," he replied.
"Nope," I corrected him. "Zillions."

He was eight and I was nine.
One day he gave me one of his brown eyes,
and I gave him one of my blue ones.
From that day onward we held hands
and played on the other side of the fence together.

When summers were young the crickets croaked
and everything smelled like lawn clippings and jasmine.
Then the leaves got brown and our hairs got gray,
and we both got laptops and cars.

When summers were young there were firefly tornadoes
and cicada supernovas,
but we're not in them anymore.
We're here, and we're big,
and the creek is a strip mall
[buy these things
they'll make you feel like you're young
like you were before everything started to hurt],
and on TV they say everything is dying.

But I've still got his hand,
and he's got mine,
and as the world does whatever it's going to do,
we play on the other side of the fence.

COFFEE

Mmm...

God.

That's good.

Perhaps,

for today at least,

I will give the universe

permission to exist

after all.

JULIAN

Because no one else would,
a white crane sits in a cage
in a sprawling city
passing messages to pigeons.

Because no one else would,
a dreamguide sits shackled for letting in light
and the world lines up to spit in his face
while heads inside screens bark and snarl.

Because no one else would,
white hairs line the floor
and the air is getting stuffy
and it's growing harder to breathe.

My great-grandchildren will scarce believe
that such a creature could have ever existed.
"That's so unfair!"
"Why'd they do that to him?"
"Why didn't the police save him?"
"Where were the grown-ups?"
"Why did that happen?"
"Why'd he have to do that?"

"Because no one else would, child,"
I will be forced to say.
"Many of us could have,
but no one else would."

GRUS GRUS

SKULLFACE COMEDIANS

"Here is a government official who's helped kill thousands of children.

Let's make jokes about his hairstyle."

"We live in a country that spends medicine money on cluster bombs.

Let's giggle about penises and vaginas."

"Your government is lying to you and the TV is helping them.

I live in a mansion but I'm just like you."

They only come out at night.

Light dances in dark rooms
across half-dead faces full of all-dead dreams
staring at advertisements between advertisements
and listening to the shrill laughter of the live studio audience
and clutching their furniture so they don't spin off the earth.

An actor sits on the chair beside the desk
and talks about a movie where actors pretend to do things
then cuts to a clip about a movie where actors pretend to do things
then cuts to a commercial about a movie where actors pretend to do things.
The host makes a joke about boobs.

The moon is not laughing.
The sky is raining the skeletons of birds.
But our hearts are real
and our flesh is made of dinosaurs and stars.
The dew collects on our eyelashes
as the horizon turns pink
and we feel our own lives
for the very first time.

Sit down, you skullfaced clown.
Tell the band to make real music,
go plant your microphone in the soil
of a garden of blossoming antiques,
set out to sea upon your desk,
and let life get a word in edgewise.

NAUGHTY LITTLE BOYS

THAT little boy's mum is going to be so upset.
He hasn't combed his hair,
and his clothes are filthy.
And what's he gone and done with his legs?
Where are your legs, little boy?
Better go and find them before your mum sees you.
Those legs are very important to her.

They sent the little boys up into the sky
and over the ocean to go play soldiers.
They gave them toy guns
full of toy bullets,
and they screamed toy screams,
and bled toy blood,
and cried toy tears,
and had toy nightmares,
and called out for their mums
in the desert.

The man on the TV keeps calling them heroes.
Don't call them that, TV man,
you'll only encourage them.
These are little boys,
and they're being very naughty.
They are worrying their mums sick
and it's time for them to go home.

Find your legs, little boy,
and go be with your mum.
Find your hands and your face too;
she'll miss those as well.
Find your mind and bring it back
from that dark, scary place.
You're not there anymore.
You are home.
Stop screaming toy screams
and crying toy tears
and go tell your mum that you've had
a bad dream.

THE MESSAGE

IN THE hidden chamber of your heart there is a god made of diamonds
writing with a worn-down pencil
in one of those notebooks with cartoon characters
that you had as a kid.

Vast cities sprawl out underneath full of people
desperately struggling not to get it all wrong.
Mechanical gargoyles have placed listening devices on their rooftops,
and the screens they are watching feed them lies.

Inside their hearts are their own gods,
some with triceratops heads,
some with wind chime bodies,
some with roots stretching down to the center of the earth,
some made entirely out of dragonfly wings,
some writing in princess notebooks,
some writing in the stars,
some writing on their skin
and on the walls in blood.

this can all end whenever we want,

in billions of languages read the words of the gods.

we can wake up whenever we are ready.

THE HAUNTERS UNDERNEATH

Do NOT discount the dissonant inexplicables
which haunt the taboo corners of your experience.
Do not dismiss the green angels
which flicker across the backs of your eyeballs.
That time when you were a child
and you saw something that couldn't have been,
 --couldn't have been–
don't spurn those.

You have seen things that are so much more real
than what you've been told to believe.
Trust your angels.
Trust the strange creature
who visited your periphery when you were small.
Not what the booming grown-ups told you
and tell you even now.

Trust your angels.
Trust your tree beasts.
Trust the haunters Underneath.

THE MAP

Know this:
You are born of the
atoms of a thousand stars
And within each atom is
a map of the universe.
Sink below the ebb and
flow of knowing and
thinking,
Tracking back through
time and space,
At once stepping into the
singularity of the moment
Where your guide to the
field appears.

It speaks:
Matter unpacks in chaotic
patterns
You are its witness
You are its will
The Bastards knew this
first
And turned their will
toward death
Using their hypnotic songs
to convince you to do the
same
Your will, til now,
has used death to solve
problems
Turn it now towards life
Turn,
Turn,
Turn,
Click.

Feel comforted, my friend. You are not alone.
Nestle your bum into the folds of the Earth.
Feel how She cherishes your body. Lean in like a
lover to the tender caress of the breeze. You are
loved, beyond measure, beyond the mealy-mouthed
judgements of the robot headthinkers, the space
aliens who will this planet to death. They are
not of this place, but you are. You are human.
You are home. Settle in.

Here, **you will find** a sword,
And a compass.
A shield,
And crown for **your** head.

Compass

Use your compass
to anchor you
to life. In that
space below the
fear and fury,
there is a watery
magnet in your
guts and it
speaks to you in
binary, yes/no.

Dowse towards truth without fear, my love, for this voiceless knowing supports all life, and in doing its work, all life supports you.

COMPASS INSTRUCTIONS: To set your compass, first hold your vision of utopia. Imagine as vividly as you can your existence on a planet where life flourishes and the will of all humans is supported and nourished. Where our valuing system boosts good things at the expense of bad, life at the expense of perpetual war, healing at the expense of perpetual sickness, the highest interest at the expense of self-interest, creativity at the expense of control. Walk around our new world in your imagination for as long as it takes before the words I WANT THIS bubble up from your core. This is the sign that your compass is ready to use.

Shield

When the Bastards come
for you, raise your karmic
shield and proclaim three
times
"I want for you what
you want for me, nothing
more, nothing less."

This ensures their will
for you turns back on
them. All this while you
projected your goodness
onto them, while they
projected their badness on
you.

Friend or foe, this shield
always works and its
effects are two-fold: it
brings good things to those
who might secretly love
you and bad things to
those who don't.

SWORD

Your sword is your words. Turn them only towards the Bastards and scythe through their lies like butter. Be relentless and unmitigated, doubtless and dauntless.

Plant your feet and say it like it's true because it is.

You have your guide, you have your compass, and you speak from the authority of the planet. Take authorship. The Bastards would have Her written out of the script if they could. You are Earth's advocate and this is a war.

Do not mute your voice for the comfort of others. Do not add insult to Her injuries by pulling your punches. You know which way we must go. Insist upon it.

CROWN

Wear your crown
at all times oh
sovereign one, and
make your first
decree:
"Only I have
dominion over me.
I am in charge of
who comes and goes,
what beliefs may
enter and what can
be expelled. I am a
champion of many
and a puppet of no
one.
"I alone rule my
kingdom."

Return here my lover to drink from the wellspring of truth and to check your field guide often. The patterns of their actions (ignore their words) are always predictable unless the miracle of your will collapses them. When we win, the guide changes. Check, check, and check again.

And then return to the battlefield, hollow yourself, and let the earth's rage at Her senseless desecration roar through you. Let it roar even though tears may prick your eyes and your body may shake with grief. Let Her rapes be yours in that moment.

Let Her voice be heard.

Hold to Her grudges and do not forgive until the pattern of behavior has collapsed. This must end. This must end now. Let it end.

Let it end now.

And so it is.

Love,

the Visitor

UTOPIA PREPPERS

WE HIDE in clockwork palaces
where the squawking screens can't find us
and plant flowers in shoes
that we found in the gutter
by the light of a jealous moon.

We do not sing about the end of days.
The end of days is for the dead.
While they bore the bone puppets
with their funeral dirges,
we have unprotected sex on top of skyscrapers
and get pregnant with woodwind virtuosos.
We paint dinosaur murals on the castles of the Bastards.
We drink blackberry wine from flamingo skulls
and lie to God.

The sea has gone still
and the birds are all watching.
We are the utopia preppers,
and we are ready for the golden age.
Tell those giant crystal elephants in the womb of time
with their mirror minds and mushroom voices
that we are hungry for our feast.

THE LUNATIC

Buried under an Everest of leather straps

fastened tightly and bolted to steel,

the madman grins

and sings of peace.

Buy Stuff

TIME

Your field of consciousness has tentacles.
It is crawling along the ceiling of eternity's womb
like an iridescent octopus in search of its final mate.

Below is bright light bursting forth
from between the cracks in your DNA.
Crow calls and whale songs fill the air.

We planted a seed in the center of this place
long ago, when we first stood erect.
We have fought wars,
placed women into cages,
invented money and built cities which touch the sky
all without disturbing its slumber.

But it's time to wake up now, tiny seed.
The phytoplankton are dying,
and the bone puppets are braying for mushroom clouds.

The click-clack-clicking of their endless marching
echoes off these city spires
in the dead of night when all good things are sleeping.
There are screaming red children in fields of oil.
Birds are falling as the air becomes poison.

It is time to wake up now, tiny seed.
Sprout now before we miss our chance.

Sprout.

Sprout.

Sprout.

THE MUSHROOM CLOUD ANGEL

A MUSHROOM CLOUD angel came to visit me one night
while I was drinking whiskey and Gatorade
and arguing with a wrong person on the internet.
It smelled like ozone and tire fires.
Its eyes stretched all the way back to the Big Bang.

"Uhh, look," I said as my vase of petunias wilted in its presence.
"Whatever this is, I'm really not ready for it.
I haven't showered, and my credit's a mess,
and I've got unresolved issues with my mother still.
Emma Carmichael next door, you should try her.
She's got her shit together.
She drives a Honda Odyssey."

There was a deep rumbling in my bones,
and the paint on the walls began to peel.
A cockroach scuttled out backwards from its hiding place.
My office supplies started to levitate,
and suddenly I knew what the creature wanted.
Why it had come to me.

"Oh," I said.
"Okay. Let me think."

I told it about how I try really, really hard
not to let any moment here go to waste.
How even if I'm just watching *The Bachelorette*
or doodling in my notepad or looking out the window,
I try to really feel every part of it.
I told it how the beauty of my lover's face makes me weep,
and how I cherish every time my kids include me in their things.
How the galahs and magpies bicker every morning
and how they make me smile while I sip my black coffee.
How I know it's spring when the magnolias blossom,
and how jasmine means summer's near.

I showed it everything I've come to adore about people;
our frailty, our ferociousness,
our relentless drive to create.
The guileless symbiosis of an elderly married couple,
the elegant awkwardness of teenagers,
the desperation of parents trying not to screw up too bad.
How thrilling it is to start again every sunrise.
How terrifying it is to fall more in love every day
with someone who can't live forever.

I invited it into my body and let it walk around in my skin
so it could feel how awesome it is to be human.
Still haven't gotten the smell out of my nostrils
or the ancient eons out of my veins.

"Well?" I asked it, my face dripping sweat,
when I'd run out of reasons to offer.
"Do we get to stay here or not?"

The mushroom cloud angel turned and walked away,
burning craters in the Carmichaels' lawn with its feet.
I don't know who else it has talked to since,
or how often we're made to answer,
but the bombs still haven't dropped.
We're all still here,
come what may.

Emma was pissed off about the grass.

MEN

THEY LINED UP over the years
to punch and kick my flower

took turns politely like good little boys
with nice clean hands

it's your turn my good man
after you sir you were here first
no no i insist
oh you are too kind

then set upon me like wolves
like apes

funneled my flesh through the secret screams of their mothers
their poor mothers who still wake up early
to put on makeup so they don't disgust their husbands
they sowed my soil with salt before my flower could bloom
then asked why i'm not like the on-screen nakeds
with sperm on their faces like war paint on the fallen
tell me i should enjoy myself more
like the ones they shat out before me

i don't know what's wrong with this one
he told the next in line
maybe her mother dropped her on her head

i held my dead flower in my eyes and wept
while making lunch wraps for the children

mowgli was raised by wolves
they taught him to run and to hunt

tarzan was raised by apes
they taught him to climb and to swing

i was raised by men
they taught me to hate my sisters

but the wind is changing
and the earth has been shaken
and there is a new topsoil now

as we kneel together
watching the sprouts emerge
we hold hands

APOCALYPSE

I STAND on the bones of every creature that has ever lived,
facing the cybertronic heirs with incomprehensible minds
who inhabit millennia henceward.
I have antlers and butterfly wings.

I open my hand and present the future with a bauble
which contains your mother's face
cooing over you when you were a baby,
and her mother's face cooing over her,
and her mother and her mother,
all the way backward through the early primates
and the reptiles and back into the oceans
to a single strand of DNA,
and then back further still
past time itself
until it comes to this.
Space angels and needle angels harmonize.
Muscular men with squid beak faces hammer upon ancient
drums.

A small child steps forward to meet me
with an open palm.
Our chests glow as one
as I forget what all the fuss was about.

A magpie sings from the heart of the universe.

IT IS TRUE

IT IS TRUE that God is dead,
and it is true that we have killed him.

But it is also true that in his bones
there are vast caverns that we have not yet explored
which are full of creatures and kingdoms.

And it is also true that in his skeletal hand
there is a key to an airship
stationed on the roof of a nearby liquor store,
and it can fly to anyplace in any universe.

And it is also true that his skull is sprouting
with a rainbow rainforest,
and kaleidoscope ivy is covering your city.

And it is also true that in your heart
there is a baby with God's eyes
who can see out of your eyes.

And it is also true that you can see that way
more and more each day if you want to.
And it is also true that we are on a mystery boat
in a sea of mystery
that is headed somewhere mysterious.

And it is also true that you are sacred
and I cherish you with every fiber of my being.

God is dead,
but we are alive,
and the next page is about to turn
like that little pause
after the final click
when the rollercoaster
completes its climb.

Click.

STRIKE THE DRUM OF THE ELEPHANT GOD

PLACE a jade crown upon the night sky, oh my daughter,
and a silver crown on each grain of sand beneath your feet.
Do not trust horny boys or polite politicians.
Trust only the hymn in your cells.
The path you must walk is as narrow as a zebra sword's edge,
and it is slippery with grandmother tears.

Find the moss-covered elephant bone, oh my daughter,
on the sea cliff where I brought you into this world,
where my labor cries mixed with the waves and the whale songs.
Strike the drum of the Elephant God with the bone
to the rhythm of the hymn in your cells.

Strike the drum for the orphans of the Calliope Wars,
and for the corpses of angels swinging from street lamps.

For the wailing trees being eaten by sheet metal locusts,

for the silent army of children with pitchforks,

for the night sky filling with deathball machines,

for the wormtoothed dragon awakening beneath the mountain,

for the puppets made of flesh dancing for the oil kings,

and for the baby who is stirring in your womb,

strike the drum, oh my daughter, strike the drum.

My cells taught you a hymn as soon as you were conceived,

and it's wiser than anything I can say to you here.

Strike the drum of the Elephant God until sunrise,

then begin making your nest as I taught you.

Your labor cries will soon mix with the cries of the
grandmothers,

and I will be cherishing you deeply, oh my daughter.

EDEN

WE HAND each new baby a briefcase and a gun
and say,
"This is how it is. Deal with it."

We tell them the lies our parents taught us,
then send them off to war in the City
where they get old and get mortgages
until they decay on their deathbeds
surrounded by acquaintances
who tell stories like,
"He built a tall tower on the east end of the City,"
or
"She wrote about clothes for a magazine."

When what we should do
(and I will scream this until my final breath)
is ask the baby,
"Well, what do *you* reckon is going on?
What's it like in there, baby,
before you've been filled with lies,
before you've been adopted by bosses and a pill-popping
spouse,
before we've painted you with oil and sold you to Amazon?

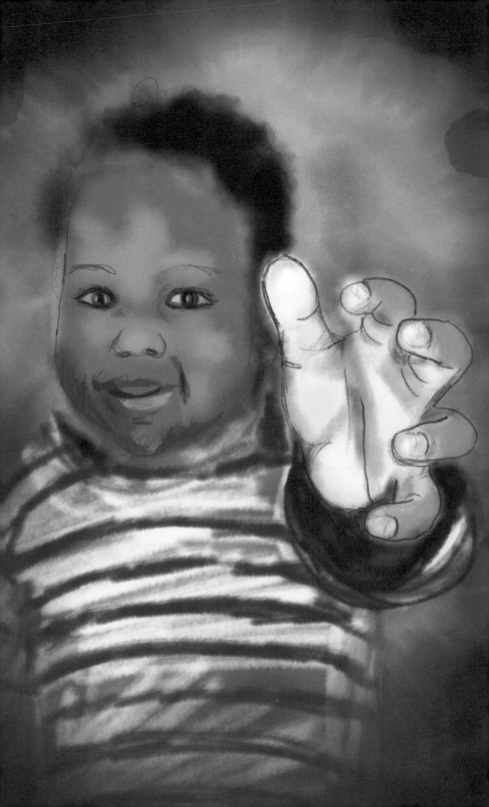

How do you look at the world with such wonder?
How do you delight in my face
when you have seen it so many times before?
How can we play again
like you play, baby?
How can we get back
to the place when the world was enthralling
and all we knew was love
before we got captured by gargoyles in the City?
Before we found ourselves clinging to screens like a life raft,
before our vision turned into gray pixels?"

What does the baby see from its cradle?
What does the space between our thoughts think about all this?
Show me your eyes as they were when they first opened
and I will walk with you back to Eden.

SPEAK

Your voice can shake the sand dunes
and make farm flowers grow on the beach.

Your voice can knock down the tall castles
of the Bastards chortling against the smoggy night sky.

They don't make you afraid of using it because it is stupid,
they make you afraid of using it because it is powerful.

So use it.

Speak.
Let your voice awaken the embryos in their cells.

Speak.
Wipe the grin off the faces of those recursive laughing buddhas
and make the very fabric of the universe look up from its TV
dinner
and take note.

Speak when your enemies tell you not to speak.

Speak when your friends and allies tell you not to speak.

Speak when your better judgment tells you not to.

Speak when every fiber of your being tells you not to.

Speak to shatter the conspiracy of silence.

Speak to end our ancient heritage of not speaking.

Speak so that others may lose their voicelessness.

Speak because only the Bastards are speaking.

Speak for the angels who are choking on chemicals.

Speak for the children sprayed red with blood.

Speak for the sea turtles drowning in plastic.

Speak for the dreamguides bulldozed and paved over.

Speak for the tree stumps bleeding crude oil.

Speak for the women trapped in small cages.

Speak for the mothers whose eyes are sedated.

Speak for the sky whose dragons have vanished.

Speak for the cities full of medicated childhoods.

Speak for the dreamers about to give up.

Speak. Speak!
We are sitting here waiting
to find out if this play will go on.

WHEN WE RAISE OUR TRUE FLAG

THERE WILL come a day
(and it won't be long now)
when the mandible-mouthed liars cease their death song,
and ivy grows over the bunkers of the Bank Boys,
and the cannons all sprout mushrooms,
and fireflies fill the air once more.

When that day comes,
we will lower the flag of the marching machine
(once used as wrapping paper for dead teenagers with rifles,
once hung over buildings full of men with red eyes,
once emblazoned upon flying robots that rained fire),
and we will raise our true flag at long last.

It will be woven from the prayers of our grandmothers
who will never see it raised but knew one day it would be.
It will be dyed in the blood of the media martyrs
who stared the Bastards in the eye and sang life songs.
It will have a traditional image of Michael the Archangel,
except instead of him stepping on the Devil
they are laughing together over a drink at the pub
while a man with a pipe looks on and smiles.
It will be based on a drawing made in crayon long ago
by a chain-smoking dryad who lurks in your brain pan.

We will all salute it in our own unique way:

with fart jokes and whale songs,

with unearthly ululations,

with runed glossolalia,

with lightning from our fingertips,

with air guitar karate,

with lava dance lovemaking,

with a single tear from someone who still misses you,

with an uplifting of the heart toward the sky.

And then we'll all curl up together

and we'll sleep unafraid

for the very first time,

and we will dream of the ones

who helped walk us home.

I WILL STAND

As THE gum tree stands in defiance
of the bushfire raging by,
as the crone stands in defiance
of death's hand day by day,
as the world stands in defiance
of poetic attempts to apprehend it,
I will stand,
O my sisters,
I will stand.

I will stand with you facing cannons,
Saudi oil wizards,
the red-eyed spy machines in our homes,
and the gargoyles in black suits.

I will stand with you facing cyborgs in riot gear,
the crooked knives of the Bank Boys,
Hollywood child eaters with tentacle teeth,
and the scoffing smileyface news platoon.

There's a morning star,
and the call of a strange gull
that labcoats had assured us was extinct.

There's a pulse in our planet only we can hear,
and it braces our legs as we stand.

Let them move their pieces into place on the board
with their clumsy metallic fingers.

Let them assemble their howling hordes on the field
with their crude crayon drawings of what they think we are.

A woman made of moons is rising from the Earth
and she will stand with us,
sisters,
she will stand.

THE END

ON THE DAY the pine bats finally burst out of the pine cones,
we will weave snapdragons and honeysuckle into our hair.
We will sing unprecedented songs
which birth unprecedented skies,
and we will laugh about the days
we thought the world was dying.

In the end only death dies,
my brown-blue-eyed baby.
This war ends
with the dying of death.

The seed sprouts.
The leaves unfurl.

THINGS THAT GROW

WALK WITH ME into the Garden wearing living clothes,
away from the dead ideas of smarmy brainiacs,
the dead towers built of Earth's last bones,
the dead machines manufacturing bullets and poison,
the dead streets paved with dead dreamguides,
and the dead voices of the death gods on television.

Walk with me into the Garden wearing living clothes,
away from moaning clerics and the books of dead men,
the mud farms and stump orchards and gargoyle gardens,
the Cyber Valley where they digitize dead minds,
the think tanks where they make our eyes turn gray,
and come play in the Garden full of things that grow.

Walk with me into the Garden wearing living clothes,
and I'll show you how deeply cherished you are,
how the wind rejoices at the touch of your flesh,
how your mind floats in a sea of undiscovered leviathans,
how plants have voices and trees are buddhas,
your infinite significance and eternal irrelevance.

Walk with me into the Garden wearing living clothes,
and get pregnant with me full of things that grow,
with baby rainforests and schools of whales,
with dragon poets forbidden from history,
with the pulsing of the Earth and the pulsing of our hearts
as we merge our cells with the Unborn.

Come with me into the Garden wearing living clothes,
and let us kneel at the feet of the things that grow.

THE LETTER

I FOUND a dead bison by the side of the freeway.
A white one, the kind that visits you in dreams
and wordlessly walks you through the wonders and horrors
of everything that lies Underneath.

It was crumbled up smashed
at the foot of a billboard for wireless service
and was partially covered in fast food wrappers.
Violets and daffodils were sprouting from its flesh.

As dark clouds gathered and wetness began to fall,
I sank down and laid upon my side.
Thinking about all the bad things.
Watching droplets wash blood from white fur.

I asked the ground,
"Why?
Why come this far
if it was just going to end like this?

With factories spewing black smoke from burnt angels
while plastic TV hosts twist their mouths into smiles?
With Raytheon revolutions and populist ecocide?
With brainwashed babies and an Amazon logo on the moon?"

I heard footsteps approaching,
but I didn't turn around.

A familiar claw reached down
and handed me a letter.

"You've been gone for decades when I needed you most," I said.
"Why come back at all?"

Air washed over me as the fucker took flight.
Never saw him again.
Didn't need to.

I opened the letter.
My tears mixed with the rain.

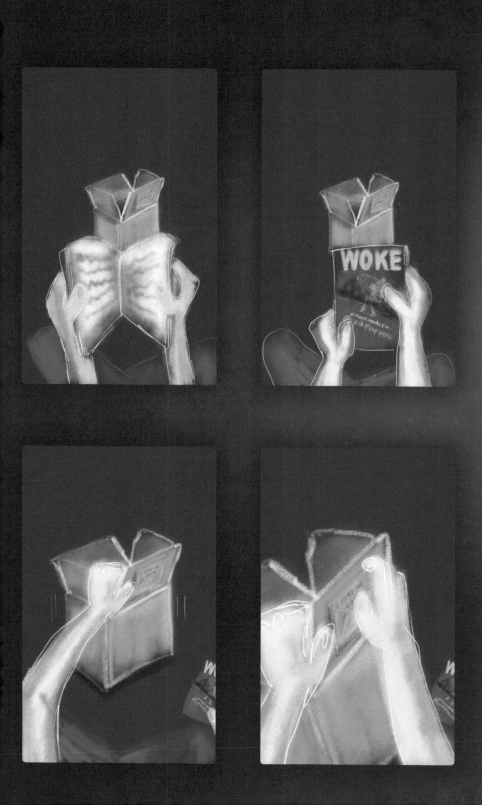

Click.